Significant Other

ISABEL GALLEYMORE's debut pamphlet, *Dazzle Ship*, was published by Worple Press in 2014. Her work has featured in magazines including *Poetry*, the *London Review of Books* and in *New Poetries VII*. In 2016 she was a poet-in-residence at the Tambopata Research Centre in the Amazon rainforest. In 2017 she received an Eric Gregory Award. She teaches at the University of Birmingham.

ISABEL GALLEYMORE

Significant

Other

CARCANET

First published in Great Britain in 2019 by
Carcanet
Alliance House, 30 Cross Street
Manchester M2 7AQ
www.carcanet.co.uk

A CIP catalogue record for this book is
available from the British Library.
ISBN 978 1 78410 711 6

Book design by Andrew Latimer
Printed in Great Britain by SRP Ltd, Exeter, Devon

The publisher acknowledges financial
assistance from Arts Council England.

Contents

For my parents

We are training each other in acts of communication we barely understand. We are, constitutively, companion species. We make each other up, in the flesh. Significantly other to each other; in specific difference, we signify in the flesh a nasty developmental infection called love.

— Donna Haraway, *The Companion Species Manifesto*

Significant Other

Ocean

Wasn't walking beside her
walking with the ocean below
when you didn't know her and wanted to?
In that heat, along that path
you hesitated

at a slug, beached
like a tiny grey whale –
thirty tonnes and seventy years
of navigating the continental shelf
assumed by this soil-scuffing inch

and what would she make of you?
The ocean blinked.
Say you took that step, or say you fell,
wouldn't she move you miles in herself?

The Starfish

creeps like expired meat –
fizzy-skinned, pentamerously-legged,
her underfur of sucking feet
shivers upon an immobile mussel
whose navy mackintosh is zipped
against the anchor of this fat paw,
this seemingly soft nutcracker who exerts
such pressure until the mussel's jaw
drops a single millimetre. Into this cleft
she'll press the shopping bag of her stomach
and turn the mollusc into broth,
haul in the goods and stumble off,
leaving a vacant cubicle,
a prayer come apart.

Once

there was a question of how close
to come to nature without being eaten,
but as the town fussed to build a fence
someone likened their hands to crows,
their stuttering heart to a common toad:
to be at one suddened the air. Rain fell
on their faces and with it they were one,
one, they said, with the rivers and stones,
one with the riverbank's wig shops of moss,
with the prickliest gorse and its bees – bright
as liquorice allsorts: at one and lost
as the woman wrapped in her lover's arms
who accidentally kisses herself.

By Ourselves

The too-hot winter sun. No cloud.
I glanced up to find
we were finally by ourselves
and had been for a while. Hadn't we

desired to be alone those times we flirted
with seeing human forms in trees?
Some evenings we gave over entirely
to making the moon one of us.

Still, it felt too fast, this intimacy:
the overhasty buds, the last few bees
finishing our sentences,
their bright cheeks turning pale.

Robin

A road sign
with a fire warning
in its breast,

a house built
for coming weather
on stilts

and taking off,
smoke,
the landing
gear pressed under.

Choosing

from eight million differently constructed hearts –
I couldn't – I chose to love them all –

the squid's triptych of pumps,
the snake's cardial sac, expanding as it eats.

To say nothing will come between us,
to stay benignly intimate was –

sometimes not calling was easier –
sometimes I'd forget to touch you
and you, and you – a natural phenomenon

dwindling – one of a dozen breakups
from the world each day –

like the others it seemed you'd just popped out
for a pint of milk and now
nothing's conjured hearing your name.

Slipper Limpet

In the double-dark of the sea at night,
a shoe of shell bears a belly-foot
that bears an appetite and so invites
a dozen to generate a vertical queue,
a carefully organised high-rise orgy
with her, its founding member,
its queen sticking to the ocean bedrock,
as smaller, younger males shuffle on top
and when she's tired of the day in day out
rut, when her gills have breathed their last,
her nearest male inherits her sex –
two moons and he's bequeathed
her duct – and yet he'll remain stuck on her
empty bone slipper, departed Cinderella.

The Ash

Like a single branch of ash
honed to the handle of an axe
and made to take the hand
of a woodsman as he throws
his body weight to fell
all the ash has sown,
I turn your words although
the line you spoke was simple

A Stranger

In one unfamiliar town
I ask a stranger where
the small red bus departs

and, told *you're almost there*
it leaves from where the elms
once stood before the road was paved,

I end up searching
for some past felling,
an old yawn in the earth –

although I'm told the only chance
of love is via falling.
How easy it is to walk past.

Into the Woods

For those who want to invest in disasters,
the INCH pack includes a sling-shot,
fishing rod and tarp. It stands for
I'm Never Coming Home.
Walk into the woods and don't look back.
I learn this from my neighbour's watching
of *Doomsday Preppers* at full volume –
her octogenarian ears believe
everyone is mumbling. On the street
she leans in uncomfortably close. They say
such impairments come by degrees.
We'll be right back with Brian's missile silo.
I give up on my book, fill the kettle.
Sunlight floods the living room;
the birds and branches of the papered walls
fade at a rate not considered change.

Kind

Being steeped
in his keeper's routine,

the owl anthropomorphises
himself upon the plinth –

if we put a female in with him
he'd still make love with the hats on our heads –

he's been here twice as long as I've been
captivated by you,

like him I don't think of myself
as possessed

until one night, loosed to the world,
I find myself expecting

everyone to be your kind
of kindness.

Goose Barnacle

An enamelled flower bud, a locket
made of shell, a lacquered fingernail
treehoused upon a wormy stalk
that wags as though to say
not quite or *not exactly so*
and this is only one of what's a fishy copse
undulating back and forth as in a gale
and asked what land they grow upon
they'd likely say no land, and asked
whose hand they reach like fingers from
they'd likely say the hand of some stray branch
that, dipping in and out of water,
persuades their beaks to open,
their feeding limbs to royally wave.

Say Heart

They say it's because I'm afraid to be alone.

What good is saying *heart*,
when you can say *heart like a little wine barrel,*
or *heart like a red squirrel.*

I am most like myself when likened.

He, for example, has made me realise
I can climb, jump between trees.

True Animal

On a dozy summer's day, a donkey magpied a lion's skin that the hunters had left to dry in the sun. What else had the donkey to do, but chameleon himself inside it? As he swanned across the paddock in his new ferocious fur, the horse began to mouse, the hare grew chicken-hearted, and the chicken hared away. How good it felt to shark among the shrimp, he thought, and let out a proud hee-haw... The daisies widened their eyes. Mid-run, the chicken stopped. The hare, and then the mouse, dared themselves to look. Finding not claws but hooves, each turned upon him and, as any true animal would, parroted a short teaching on natures true and fox.

Seahorse

Isn't it shocking how he speaks for her?
His thin voice wavering across the restaurant –
she'll have the cod artichoke bake.

A giggle of bubbles comes from behind them:
a fish tank curtained with seagrass
where a seahorse is tying itself
to one of these slim, tweedy forms

like a hand shaping itself inside another's
the way my hand tucks into his
like a difference pretending it's not.

Together

the heart aflame no longer
shines any light on love
because they are always together –

because they are always together
it's hard to see them apart
like the blade in the blade of grass –

two lovers grew so close they became
too fluently familiar
having lost what makes fire fire.

Day

Having lived this long with one another,
we know day's 'face', day's 'hands' so very well;
the way it touches and likes to be touched;
can, in the most part, read its 'mind',

so when we hear that day is only playing along
that day has a plan to abandon us
we brush it off as gossip. After all,
the orange juice carton pours out orange,

birds gently carry on birdsplaining themselves,
under the trees of our tree-lined streets
a few of us gather without exception,
our talk of the weather still small.

At First

The seasons grew untidy;
the months filled up with rain.
At first it came soft as a sheep.
Inside the sheep a wolf, of course
inside the wolf a man intent
on acting out his tale.

No Inclination

It came to light that mountains were some
of the least despondent land formations,
that a surprising number of gales
didn't know what it was to howl.
The woebegone voice of the willow
confirmed it had no reason to weep.
Accordingly, schoolchildren were instructed
to rip up their books, releasing
alligators from their anger,
bees from their busyness,
cats from their curiosity…
while one neighbourhood didn't see any harm
pulling the sun closer to inspect.
It couldn't be denied: that fiery mass
possessed no inclination to smile.
Household after household poured
whiskey-cokes to toast the news,
the ice melting fast in their drinks.

Limpet & Drill-Tongued Whelk

Across the rockpool floor, a limpet grazes –
a stray magician's cup,
moon-textured, the shape of light
pointing through frosted glass.
It is a modest party hat
in which something like a head resides
oblivious of this dog whelk
that pads against the thick, still brine
and climbs upon the limpet –
an ornate seat upon an elephant.
Carnivorous mollusc, tiny fracking rig
clocking in with its drill-tongue, clutching
as the limpet rises from the stone,
to become half-mushroom, half bucking bronco.

Difficult Cup

after Wu Hao's 'Duke Cups'

The china cup is frilled at the rim
like tired lace and all over it
ceramic tentacles extend
to whisper *if you drink me that way*
I'll poke your eye out, you
can't quite press your fingers here
your lips – like walking a mountain ridge
at night with some romantic
ideal ahead, you are not
not figuring each step among
the rocks –
there's want and caution
caught in you and a new
vocabulary of pouting to be learnt.

Spirit Human

Let's do it like they do on the discovery
channel the prowess of the lion, the deer's
intuition tells us animals don't like to be shoes
because animals love to be shoes
gummy sweets, similes, like people
they long to be airlifted from being themselves
amongst candles, cheap incense, the hum
of a fridge and the chatter of next door's
animals, even when dog-tired, will pay
attention and skill are needed in modelling
themselves after retail assistants and chefs
after penniless artists and presidents, after
all animals need to discover themselves

The Scrotum Frog

The day is unendangeredly bright
when you kiss your lover in the hope
he'll turn into a frog. All the windows

are open and it's still too hot in the house.
The lake? you ask your loose-skinned one,
pink-grey as that old part of himself.

Somewhere you've read, like many others,
that the best love is the unattainable kind:
a dreamy stranger with a wordless mouth

sits among the reeds and crisp packets.
For weeks, you meet by the shoreline
when it's cool, when the sun is a come-to-bed eye.

Then he's gone. One and then another
speedboat snore across the dirty water.
You close the windows, draw the curtains.

You fall asleep and dream of him
with his brothers in the lake like men
in a changing room; sweaty, doling out nicknames –
Sac Magique, Sir Chicken Skin.

I Keep You

at a difference:
a thought I won't allow myself
to think for thinking
it's a matter of time
till you, a cargo
ship of foreign goods,
cross my kitchen table
like a butter dish.

Nectaries

I.

The shape of the dark
when she opens her lips

on the lilac's frilly cock of pollens

Each identity:
an allusion to the other

A furzy pubis
on the Milk and Honey

The reciprocal capture
between bee and flower

2.

It wasn't only the orchids
masquerading as bees,
the flowers making promises
of phony nectaries,

I also thought of the wasp –
the way she's known to hatch
her important dreams
on the caterpillar's back.

Of course I thought of the mantis,
I thought of the cuckoo too –
still nothing helped explain
what I had done to you.

3.

A note on the petal
from the last nectar-robber –
I was here and drained the lot.

Others near and read
and reel sharply back
into the sky.

No matter, what he wrote
wears off – one flower
clothed in yellow claws

needs one full turn of Earth,
another dressed in blue
just minutes to re-self.

Eye & Sight

When I was a stay-at-home eye,
sight would often leave me

like water lifting from a lake
he mixed with other bodies.

I guessed he loved, the way clouds love,
the free and godly view

and didn't know the more he pledged
himself to this pursuit

the more he'd fall straight back to me.
Like any eye, I sank

all his disclosures through a nerve
streaming towards the dark.

Spiny Cockle

From their metre-deep sandy resorts
the waves have raised these hard orbs:
clenched like cement hedgehogs
they wear their ribs inside out
and pricked with a white picket fence
to keep their soapdish interiors –
their lattice-gill-slither selves –
from the crunch of an oystercatcher's kiss
or the orange fog of this starfish
that causes one cockle to buckle and let
its long pink foot slip like a leg
from the slit of its crenulated skirt:
soft pogo on which it floppy-leaps
away across the wet desert.

The Wingless Wasp

It seems that 'one' is fated
to be another's 'half' –
what sense in this construction –

wingless cliché on a stem
waiting for her man
to lift her from her feet

because the fruit's too high to sip –
rising between the branches
I say 'they' and you say 'it'.

Worm

And like so many times before,
the worm catches the bird
by quietly and cleanly
pushing from the dirt.

Standing *en pointe*, the worm
attacks his yellow beak;
jabs so hard the bird's almost
lifted from his feet.

Professional, silk-suited, she
requires just one stroke
to twist herself around
the silver hook inside his throat.

The worm, both rein and rider,
now being safely tied,
gives a final twitch
and hoists the bird into the sky.

The New World

It's leaf-nose o'clock. The pink toes are poised.
In the dark understory, the wolf with eight legs
dines on the harlequin's long eyes.
A whip on the floor, a whip on the limb.
The bush-master waits.
An untouchable lobster
fattens upon the leaf litter.
Some body is calling for mother, mother.
Some body munches on sphinx.
For all their splashing in the figgeries
the earless family can't wake
the kissy sounds from sleep.

Rainforest Spelled Backwards Is Lustful

Amongst the saplings and small ferns, you
can't help but see a skirt of penises
prodding into the earth, the roots are short and
unobtrusive warts allow the tree to suck
the air is steamy and I become self-
conscious of this other body, I don't know where to
'look! the erotic palm tree!' the guide announces
quietly I question if he's made the name
up above the other trunks, the palm grows
pregnant, or so indigenous peoples are said
to believe in desire is surely to believe in
hunger leads monkeys to the topmost fronds
because the drupes are ripe one drops
like an earring among the leaves I am very small

Harvest

for Frances

After stripping the branches of berries
the robin held a handful of seeds
in her stomach: the robin carried a tree
– in fact she secretly sowed a whole forest –
a store of bows and arrows and shields.
Years found the bird had planted a battle,
her tiny body had borne the new king.

Men looked up to the skies and blessed
or blamed the planets moving overhead.
A blackbird, meanwhile, started to pick
at the fruit both armies had left.

Tended

A hot afternoon and tiredness has him
turning to the garden for fresh air
where he spills coffee and goes to swear – and swears

because she is, of course, in bed
and not about to come downstairs.

Beyond the oak, in full sun the fields
of maize grow rainbows as the tractors spray.

Beneath her curtained window, in their plot,
tended by his hands these days,
a bee is abandoning itself on his abandoned spade.

From the corner of his eye, he sees her
raise her claw as if to wave.

How long now? He blows away the steam and sips.

The struggling buzz of the bedside bell.

It no longer seems like myth: to live
like bee to blossom, blossom fruit;
within an hour of each other, leave.

Nuptials

One day, downhill from the farmer's field,
I, a frog, married a drain,
married its cool and its damp,
web-wed its steely gills,
its shaggy walls and mind of flies:
to which the drain gave consent
silently adding its nuptials.

So overgrown with green
and happy clamminess,
on the eve of our first year
a fifth foot bulbed from my skin
with something of the pressure and shape
of a cork being eased
from a bottle of champagne.

Crickets

With this breeze
the springing crickets explore
an astronaut's grasp of gravity. Flung

like the second half of a metaphor
I look back and there I am
and here, too

differently. Uncrossable
space between myselves.
A crowd

of moonwalkers tittering
and not one cricket
on the breeze.

Strawberry & Ship-of-War

They plucked each other out of the air
        the way you might pluck any two words
and now they've as little between them
        as a *strawberry* and a *ship-of-war* –
she asks me how to make this work,
        the last six months she's been aware
a strawberry is like a warship because
        neither are similar, they've really
nothing to say to each other;
        easier to paint the small fruit
with smaller uniforms, union jacks –
        what's tying them together except
their obliviousness concerning
        the instincts which govern them,
their being aphrodisiacs.

Barnacles

Think of them now – *Invincible, Endeavour*
well-endowed with this swamping thatch
of teeth, this citadel of calciferic bedsits
their single occupants can never leave –
what is it about November that washes
urge into this one's sinus-heart
eliciting his wily pipette
that with its several accordion folds
stretches beyond his stuck-fast self
to become a proboscis, a blind man's stick
abristle with sniffing as it wavers and knocks
against his lady-neighbour's operculum doors
only to break off like part of the rigging
the moment the mood no longer takes him.

False Limpet

Armour tailored to an elbow's point and wrinkle, and with that same toothy colour: a *False Limpet* by this encyclopedia – as if it were never itself, only the imitation of something else. It's the way you hold your mouth so tight; you're so like someone I once met – but O, watch this slip from the rock with a splashy unclinginess.

Shadow Tale

In the tree, down the trunk,
on the curb and then running
in front of a car.

Experience has taught me
if it doesn't work out with you,
if I don't see you again

along comes another
I can't tell apart.

I'm Doing You an Injustice

It's like I've invited you to a party
of people I know but you don't –
I see you fitting into the erratic
spaces between people talking
till I only see parts of you
like the nude beneath the willow
who doesn't look quite herself
dappled by the shadowings
from what is given light first.

Succession

A gap in the trees
where a fig takes hold
and capuchin monkeys
after the fruit;

like bold picaflores
who venture for nectar,
leaf-cutter ants
for their leaves;

gold-miners flit
between heliconias,
workmen methodically
take down the trees.

Luminescent

for Sharanya

I believed I was like
the rockpool's tuft
of ale-brown algae
that exclusively blushed
luminescent blue
when poked by that
boy with a stick
who was really hoping
to poke a starfish –
only to find
I can, all night,
by any breath's ripple,
perform my own borealis.

Crab

Sublittoral place in which this crab sits
like the lid of a pie, its crimped edge
rests upon a mixture of pincers, legs –
two black dactyls headline the others
dressed in the fizz and stubble of brick.
It's these bone clothes the crab outgrows
the way song, lifting a decibel, bursts
a glass, there's some civil upheaval
as the crab thwarts the fortlet of itself
and pauses for a minute, out-of-body,
a faded, vulnerable replica,
a soft ball of milk with milk's film skin
soon to search for a hiding place
for the time it will take to scab over.

Significant Other

A cloud takes on the shape of a tortoise.

The tortoise can never
repay the gesture. Unashamedly,

its owner once believed that it answered

hello in its reptilian hiss
as she once believed that he, who delighted

her body, delighted her body

only. Did the creature ever think
a thought her way?

The tortoise snaps its tortoisey jaws

eating all that's laid on
without looking up.

Examples Include Celine Dion's 'My Heart Will Go On'

The toy ring with little kitten's face
loves the world so very much!
Child's room, roadside, ocean floor...
decade after decade, it can't tear itself away!
When the world comes home tired,
the toy ring with little kitten's face
is the pink and heart-shaped post-it note,
is the bunch of petrol-station flowers
one person gives another as they imitate
the hard-wearing infatuation
of the toy ring with little kitten's face.

Oh people in their cars and kitchens
singing of forever and always...
Really! You have to feel for them.

Are We There Yet?

So we may move beyond our park
(with its yellowed trees,
the taciturn ice cream vendor
whose flavours now seem bland)
a bridge is designed and built.
Like someone approaching
a stranger in a bar
I'm no photographer, but I can picture
me and you together,
we stride across; the rails
already bushy with brassy
locks that love the bridge that links
this part of earth with the next

Notes

The use of the phrase, 'Significant Other' is influenced by Donna Haraway's discussion of 'significant otherness' in *Notes of a Sportswriter's Daughter* and *The Companion Species Manifesto*.

In 'Choosing', the number of eight million refers to the estimated 8.7 million species currently living on Earth.

'Say *Heart*' alters a line from 'Lying' by Richard Wilbur.

The first line of 'Spirit Human' is taken from 'The Bad Touch' by The Bloodhound Gang.

Both italicised sections of the first poem of 'Nectaries' come from Isabelle Stengers's theory of 'reciprocal capture' in *Cosmopolitics I*.

'Spirit Human' and 'Rainforest Spelled Backwards is Lustful' are written after Matthea Harvey's style of lineation in *Pity the Bathtub Its Forced Embrace of the Human Form*.

Acknowledgements

Thanks are due to the following publications in which these poems first appeared: *Poetry*, *London Review of Books*, *Wild Court*, *PN Review*, *Stand*, *The Compass*, *Hotel*, *And Other Poems*, 'Triptych' (Guillemot Press), *Entanglements: New Ecopoetry* and *New Poetries VII*. 'Difficult Cup' won The London Magazine Poetry Prize in 2015, 'Limpet & Drill-Tongued Whelk' won The Basil Bunting Prize in 2016 and several poems received The Girton Prize in the same year. 'Together', 'Harvest', and 'I'm Doing You an Injustice' appeared in the pamphlet, *Dazzle Ship* (Worple Press, 2014).

I am immensely grateful to the Society of Authors for an Eric Gregory Award in 2017, to the Arts Council England for a grant in 2016 and to the Hawthornden Foundation for a Fellowship in 2012. My sincere thanks to the Charles Causley Trust, Cathy Rozel Farnworth (host of the Roger and Laura Farnworth Arts Residency in partnership with the Bodmin Moor Poetry Festival) and Crackington Manor for giving me spaces in which to write the beginnings of this collection, and to Trelex, Tambopata Research Centre and Rainforest Expeditions for giving me the opportunity to be resident poet in the Amazon.

Huge thanks and love to Phil Child, Jenna Clake, Emily Hasler, Sharanya Murali, Robert Peake, Declan Ryan, Ruth Stacey and Luke Thompson.